G000097669

Microwave Combination Ovens

Your Questions Answered

Microwave Combination Ovens

Your Questions Answered

Jan Harris

ANGELL EDITIONS
Newton Abbot, Devon

First Published April 1987

Line illustrations by Evelyn Bartlett

Printed in England
by Vine & Gorfin Limited, Exmouth
for Angell Editions Limited
39 Coombeshead Road, Newton Abbot, Devon

British Library Cataloguing in Publication Data
Harris, Jan
  Microwave combination ovens: your questions answered.
  1. Microwave cookery
  I. Title
641.5′882   TX832

ISBN 0 948432 45 4

Contents

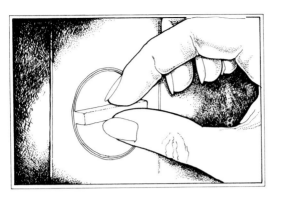

Are Microwaves Safe?

Whilst the question of safety in microwave oven use has largely been answered satisfactorily, queries are still raised daily by consumers. The questions in this section are most typical, and should allay all fears.

1   Q. Are microwave ovens built to a higher degree of safety nowadays?

    A. Yes. Most machines have six different safety factors. If in doubt always look for British Electrical Approval Board (BEAB) approval or the British Standards Institution's 'kite-mark'.

2   Q. Does microwave leakage cause cancer?

    A. No. Obviously microwaves are a form of radiation and in quantity would be very harmful; but the very, very miniscule amount of leakage from a microwave oven is insufficient to be harmful, and indeed is less than emitted from a colour TV.

3   Q. Is it possible to put one's hand in the microwave whilst it is working?

    A. No. Microwaves are automatically switched off when the 'door-open' operation is touched.

4   Q. What happens to the microwaves? Are they still in the food after cooking?

    A. Microwaves are little pulses of energy which are used up on the heating process and disappear completely. To prove this, place a light-bulb in $\frac{1}{2}$ cup of milk and switch your microwave oven on HIGH for $1\frac{1}{2}$ min. The bulb will light up. Switch off the machine and the bulb will go out, proving no microwaves are left in the milk.
    IMPORTANT: prolonged or repeated use of this test will damage the machine.

5   Q. Why don't the microwaves pass through the door?

    A. Microwaves travel in straight lines bouncing off the cavity walls but not moving in a forward direction. There is a very fine metal mesh in the door to deflect the rays in an improbable isolated situation.

6 Q. Will the door leak in time?

A. No. During manufacture the door is opened and closed 30,000 times on test machines.

7 Q. Is it dangerous to put metal inside a microwave combination oven?

A. *Some* manufacturers recommend it, but it would damage the machine if the instruction manual clearly states NO metal.

8 Q. If I accidentally left a metal spoon in a dish during cooking on microwave mode, would it damage the machine?

A. All of us at some time or another leave metal in the oven. Isolated incidents will not do much harm but in prolonged contact with the microwave metal will, in time, damage the oven.

9 Q. Should the oven be switched off at the plug every night?

A. No. In many machines this would mean setting the clock daily, and is unnecessary unless the microwave is being left for long periods such as holidays.

10 Q. Should food be removed from the microwave combination oven as soon as the machine switches off?

A. Yes, when using combination or convection. It doesn't matter one way or the other when only using microwaves, which continue to cook for a few moments only. Food will then cool naturally whether in the microwave oven, or out of it.

11 Q. Does the microwave oven automatically switch off?

A. Yes, immediately the door-release operation is touched.

12 Q. What happens to the microwaves when the door is opened?

A. They are already 'used up' such is the speed o microwave activity.

13 Q. I noticed steam escaping from the outside of the oven door. Is the microwave safe to use?

A. Yes. Steam escapes by travelling around the edges of the door. Microwaves travel in straight lines only, and therefore cannot escape.

14 Q. Does the outside casing of a microwave combination oven get very hot?

A. Yes but not as hot as a conventional oven casing.

15 Q. What harm would be caused if someone inadvertently started a microwave oven by mistake?

A. If, for a prolonged period, microwaves are bounced into the cavity without moisture to work on, or 'use' them up, the microwave oven's magnetron could be damaged. Always leave a cup of water inside the oven when not in use.

16 Q. When using the microwave mode, why don't plastic dishes melt?

A. Because microwaves pass straight through any substance other than metal so there is no direct heat on the dishes; only heat transferred from fooc being cooked.

17 Q. Is it safe to use metal spoons when stirring food?

A. Yes, but do not leave cutlery in the oven during cooking.

8   *Q.* Would it be better if I used wooden or plastic spoons?

A. Neither of these would adversely affect the oven if accidentally left inside during cooking, though possibly the plastic spoon would melt slightly and distort.

9   *Q.* Will oven gloves protect my hands from microwaves?

A. There is no need to protect your hands, as there is no contact with microwaves. When the microwave oven door is opened the microwaves have already disappeared.

20   *Q.* Will I need oven gloves?

A. Yes for convection or combination modes.

21   *Q.* What would happen to the food if there was a power failure?

A. Exactly the same as cooking conventionally. The food would be partially cooked. When power became restored cooking could be completed, but with a higher degree of safety since microwaves sterilize food instantly.

22   *Q.* Is it all right to use an adaptor in an electric wall-point to which a microwave oven is connected?

A. No. Allow one plug per socket for the microwave.

23   *Q.* Are microwave combination ovens safe for children to use?

A. On microwave mode they are safer than conventional cookers. On combination and convection modes the same safety precautions as a conventional oven will apply.

24 *Q*. Does the timer automatically switch off at the end of each cooking-cycle?

A. Yes.

25 *Q*. Can microwaves affect the workings of a heart-pacemaker?

A. Heart-pacemakers have been known to be affected by microwaves, but there are many users who are not affected. Check with your medical specialist.

26 *Q*. Does a microwave oven need regular servicing?

A. Yes. Every two years.

27 *Q*. What would a service consist of?

A. Checking and testing all main parts, including the magnetron.

Buying a
Microwave
Combination Oven

*When choosing any new cooking appliance
there are many considerations. More so with
a microwave combination oven, as often it is
the first introduction to microwave cookery.
The following information will enable the
consumer to choose the correct type of cooker
for specific needs.*

28 *Q.* What is a microwave combination oven?

A. An electric fan oven and microwave oven combined.

29 *Q.* I have always understood that microwaves don't brown food. How does the microwave combination oven differ and why does the food brown as normal?

A. Microwaves heat food from within by agitating molecules of moisture; not by using direct heat. A combination cooker uses electricity to create direct heat which is circulated around the oven by a fan, in addition to microwaves.

30 *Q.* I would like to reorganise my kitchen and dispose of my conventional cooker. Which type microwave oven would you recommend?

A. There are models available that have the facilities of both the microwave and the electric fan-assisted oven. Look for one that combines the two together as the time saving is tremendous. Such a machine will roast a 1.4kg (3lb) joint of meat and potatoes for four (beautifully crisped and roasted), in 45 min from a cold start! It may be used as an independent microwave cooker, as a convection hot-air fan-assisted oven, or successfully combines both together. Also, some machines have grills.

31 *Q.* Is there a microwave browning oven that can be programmed to switch on in the users absence from home?

A. Not to my knowledge.

32 *Q.* How could I grill food if I had no other means of cooking than a microwave combination oven?

A. Very good simulated grilling results may be obtained by using the convection mode. Preheat the cavity for 5–10 mins then place food on the rack provided and cook food using convection only.

33 Q. What are the main areas of difference in microwave combination ovens?

A. Price largely dictates; stainless steel or acrylic linings; auto sensor facility; auto weight defrosting. In addition there is the speed of cooking and the ability to use metal dishes. Some are more user-friendly than others.

34 Q. What could I cook more easily in an oven with variable power that I cannot cook in my machine with COOK/DEFROST?

A. Milk puddings, all cheaper cuts of meat, joints, stews, casseroles.

35 Q. If I buy a microwave combination oven to replace my existing cooker, will I need a hob?

A. With organization you could manage without; but most people prefer to have conventional cooking as well.

36 Q. If I decided not to have a hob what other electrical equipment would be useful as a back-up?

A. A toaster, a deep-fat fryer and a mini-boiler for eggs (the type used in hotel bedrooms for quick cups of coffee).

37 Q. If I buy a microwave combination oven, would it make sense to retain my existing microwave oven?

A. Yes. There would be no need for a conventional oven and the two microwave ovens would allow simultaneous cooking of different dishes.

38 Q. I am considering replacing my basic microwave oven, which is 500-watt power. Since higher-power ovens are more expensive, would they be more 'efficient'?

A. No. The actual power governs the speed at which food can be cooked. Newer machines are more efficient because of turntables, variable power and programmability.

39   *Q.* When using my microwave oven I can only bake one half of a Victoria sponge at a time. If I buy a combination cooker is the same method used?

    A. No. Combination cookery is similar to conventional cookery. Dishes may be arranged in the oven utilizing both shelf and turntable.

40   *Q.* I have an auto sensor microwave oven, and would like similar facilities on a microwave combination oven. Is there such an appliance available?

    A. Yes.

41   *Q.* My microwave oven has an automatic defrosting facility that works by programming the weight and type of food. Is there a microwave combination oven with this facility?

    A. Yes.

42   *Q.* What is auto-weight defrosting?

    A. The machine is programmed with the type of food and weight to be defrosted. From then on it is automatic.

43   *Q.* Does a microwave combination oven have a defrost facility?

    A. Yes. Plus other variable power settings.

44   *Q.* Some types of microwave combination ovens have a mass of buttons, others just a few. Are all the functions essential or are the less complicated ovens likely to do the same job with less fuss?

    A. Obviously some machines are more comprehensive than others. Generally, the more buttons the more automation the oven will have and less for you to work out. The choice is either to master microwave cooking oneself or to master a complicated machine that has mastered it for you.

45 *Q.* What is variable power?

A. If microwave mode is selected, variable power is the name given to the function of different heat settings. If HIGH is selected, the machine is switched on fully for the time given. If ROAST is selected, the machine switches on for 50 sec and switches off for the remaining 10 sec in every minute of the time selected, thereby food does not get quite so hot as when using full power. For DEFROST the machine is on for 30 sec, off for 30 sec in every minute, and so on.

46 *Q.* Are machines with automatic settings superior to manual machines?

A. Some are, some aren't. Make quite sure, before buying, just what all those settings are for, and whether your household requires them all. Generally, a manual machine is better for someone who is around the house for a good proportion of the day.

47 *Q.* What are the advantages of a touchbutton microwave oven over a manual machine?

A. Generally speaking, programmability. To be able to instruct the machine to control itself without having to be in the vicinity. Rather like the benefits of an automatic washing machine.

48 *Q.* What does auto-sensor mean?

A. The machine determines cooking time automatically from the pressure of a touch-pad by measuring heat and moisture rising from food whilst cooking. Hence the term auto-sense.

49 *Q.* Is there a microwave combination oven available with a hob attached?

A. No. Siemens produce a microwave-only oven with a hob fitment on the top.

50 *Q.* Using a microwave combination oven, what are the energy savings over a conventional oven?

A. Microwave mode—up to 75% reduction and Combination mode—up to 50% reduction.

51 *Q.* What is the importance of the cubic capacity of a microwave combination oven?

A. The larger the cavity, the bigger the turkey at Christmas!

52 *Q.* I understand the most important feature of a microwave oven is the door. Which type is best?

A. A metal-edged door, rather than plastic, set into a deep recess.

53 *Q.* Is a turntable really necessary?

A. It saves a lot of time opening and closing the door to turn the food. Also, it avoids the need to be in the vicinity of the kitchen during cooking.

54 *Q.* Is a stainless steel interior better than acrylic?

A. Yes, stainless steel is easier to clean and will last much longer.

55 *Q.* Will I need a cooker point?

A. No. A 13 amp power point is all that is required.

56 *Q.* Are there any special considerations regarding the site of a combination cooker?

A. Do not place too near a conventional cooker. Allow space around the unit for free air flow. Check manufacturer's installation instructions.

57 *Q.* Does it matter where my machine is situated in the kitchen? Can it be put in the larder for instance?

A. Wherever you find is most convenient will be suitable for the microwave oven, provided sufficient air is allowed to circulate.—25–30mm (1–1$\frac{1}{4}$in) around the outer casing is acceptable.

58 Q. If I fit my microwave on a shelf under a food cupboard in which I keep breakfast cereals, would the steam from the oven affect them?

A. No. There is not sufficient steam escaping from the door to do this.

59 Q. Is the top of a medium height fridge a safe place to stand a microwave browning oven?

A. No. The heat from the oven could affect the fridge temperature.

60 Q. How simple is it to 'build in' a microwave combination oven to a unit?

A. Provided the electrical supply is available, very simple. If the kitchen fitter cannot supply a fix-in surround, most microwave-oven manufacturers sell them.

61 Q. Are there neatening strips produced for wall fitting and units?

A. Manufacturers produce purpose-made fixing kits, available to order.

62 Q. Are some microwave ovens noisier than others?

A. Yes. Try to see a variety of machines working before buying, to enable the best choice to be made.

63 Q. Is there a machine produced that has a right-hand door opening?

A. Not to my knowledge.

64 Q. How does a microwave combination oven save time on washing up?

A. There are no saucepans. Food is often prepared and eaten in the same dish and there are no burned-in stains when using the microwave mode.

65 *Q*. Compared to conventional cooking, is the food as high in nutrients after cooking in the microwave combination oven?

A. Higher. Food is cooked so quickly that there is less loss of nutrients.

66 *Q*. How would I know when the microwave oven has finished cooking?

A. A bell or buzzer informs you.

67 *Q*. I am deaf and cannot hear the bell 'ping' at the end of a cooking cycle. Would I still be able to use a microwave oven?

A. Yes. The light inside the machine switches on whilst food is cooking and off when the machine has finished.

68 *Q*. Is a white cabinet more costly?

A. It is not normally.

69 *Q*. Is there more to go wrong with a combination oven compared to a microwave-only model?

A. Yes, because there are more parts but ovens are very reliable.

70 *Q*. How long a guarantee is given with a microwave oven?

A. Usually 2–3 years on the magnetron; 1 year on parts and labour.

71 *Q*. Is there an optional extended warranty?

A. An additional option of service cover for up to 5 years is usually available at varying prices. Generally the microwave specialist engineer's premium is slightly higher, but better value as most cover all parts inclusive of glass turntable, tray and light-bulb.

72　*Q.* If a combination oven developed a fault how long would it take to repair?

　　A. Microwave specialist repairers give precedence to such users and would normally fix it within 24 hours.

73　*Q.* As there are more working parts is it more expensive to service a microwave combination oven than a microwave-only oven?

　　A. Yes. Though generally the same call out fee and hourly rate apply.

74　*Q.* Is there a service contract available for a microwave combination oven?

　　A. Yes. The dealer or microwave service agent can arrange.

75　*Q.* What is the expected life of a microwave combination oven?

　　A. A microwave combination oven should last for many years. As with other appliances, all parts are replaceable over a reasonable period.

76　*Q.* What is likely to go wrong?

　　A. The magnetron. It is the most important part of a microwave oven and is generally guaranteed for up to three years.

77　*Q.* Could I repair the oven myself?

　　A. No. Always use a qualified service engineer.

78　*Q.* Could I buy parts to do so if I wished?

　　A. Yes, but be warned!

79 *Q*. Are there any British manufacturers of microwave combination ovens?

A. Not at the moment. The magnetron, which is the fundamental part of any microwave oven is always manufactured in Japan. Therefore, there is no 100% British domestic microwave oven though some are assembled here.

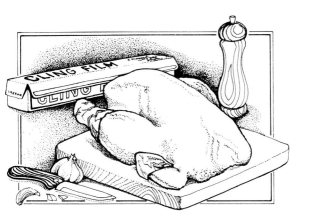

Cooking Tips

A microwave combination oven is easier to master than a microwave-only oven. Food is presented traditionally and roasts can be cooked in one dish in the normal manner. However, there is still some trial and error, and the following points will reduce the early stage problems.

80 *Q.* Can I make tea in a microwave oven?

A. Yes. Boil water in a ceramic pot and make tea as normal but it will take longer than using an electric kettle.

81 *Q.* Can I make filter coffee in the microwave oven?

A. Yes. There are special coffee makers for the microwave oven. Alternatively make it conventionally and reheat by the cup for approximately 2 min.

82 *Q.* Is it possible to fry food in the microwave oven?

A. Yes. Using the browning dish, which is a frying-pan substitute.

83 *Q.* Will it make toast?

A. Only on the models with a grill

84 *Q.* Can I deep fat fry?

A. No. The temperature of the fat cannot be safely controlled.

85 *Q.* Can I make sauces in the microwave oven?

A. Yes. Refer to recipe book

86 *Q.* Can I melt a jelly tablet in the microwave oven?

A. Break jelly tablet into cubes. Microwave HIGH 30–45 secs, make up with cold water. Leave to set

87 *Q.* I make a quick curry on my conventional stove top, using cooked chicken. Could I make the same dish in the microwave?

A. Yes. Cook onions first, then add remaining ingredients. Cook on HIGH for about half the conventional cooking time.

Q. Is it possible to cook poppodums in the microwave browning oven?

A. Yes. Brush with melted oil or fat and heat on microwave HIGH setting until ready.

Q. How would I cook prepared boil-in-the-bag meals?

A. Snip the corner of the bag and put the bag into a dish to catch spillage. Cook on HIGH without first defrosting. Trial and error is needed for timing; try half the conventional time to start with.

Q. Would I need to use browning spices?

A. Not unless you wished to use them to flavour food.

Q. What cannot be cooked in a combination oven?

A. A boiled egg. The inside of the egg expands with the heat; the egg bursts its shell with a mini explosion which could cause damage.

Q. The recipe book supplied with my combination oven gives alternative methods of cooking bacon rashers—either combination or microwave mode. Which is best?

A. In this instance microwave cooking will be cheaper.

Q. How do I decide which mode to use?

A. *Combination*—Roast meats, roast potatoes, Yorkshire puddings, scalloped potatoes, pastry, cakes, bread and apple crumble or for anything requiring a crusty top.

Convection—small cakes, frying eggs on Pyrex plate, warming plates etc.

Microwave—vegetables, milk puddings, fruit, sauces, scrambled eggs, poached eggs; reheating cooked foods; defrosting frozen food; melting chocolate, jam, jelly cubes or frozen fats.

94   *Q*. When should I use the metal rack supplied with my oven?

A. When using metal (if manufacturer recommends use of metal) such as pies and pastries in tin foil.

The rack allows convected hot air to reach base of the dishes, where microwaves cannot penetrate.

The rack is also useful when cooking two separate dishes e.g. roast with Yorkshire pudding.

95   *Q*. My machine has an auto-sensor and the instructions state quite clearly that I should cover all dishes with plastic wrap and not pierce a hole. Why?

A. The sensor works by measuring humidity and moisture present in the food during cooking, and it is necessary to 'seal' the dish for the sensor to work accurately. Plastic wrap is a very good medium for this, but it is generally agreed that a three-piece dome-dish set does the job more efficiently.

96   *Q*. Is it safe to use cling-film on microwave mode?

A. There has been a health warning about the possible dangers of ingestion of chemicals released during cooking. It is recommended that plastic wrap which is free of P.V.C. be used.

97   *Q*. When converting my own recipes I cannot make a success of the temperature settings. Food ends up overdone or pale and anaemic. Can you give me some guidelines?

A. Only use the highest temperature setting for foods that require browning and crisping quickly, but will not become spoiled by intense heat, e.g. roast potatoes, Yorkshire pudding, jam tarts. Reduce to medium temperature such items as pies since the filling takes longer to cook than the pastry crust. Medium setting is the safest bet when in doubt.

Q. When does one use the convection-only mode?

A. For small cakes or tarts, biscuits etc. because using the combination method would cook the food before the convected hot air was hot enough to brown. Preheating the oven prior to combination speeds up the cooking time.

Q. Can I clean the trivet and wire racks in a dishwasher?

A. Yes.

0 *Q.* Does a combination oven get dirty?

A. Yes. There will be fat splashes, but as the machine is in use for less time, the stains are less burned-in and can be easily removed after cooking.

1 *Q.* How should I clean a combination cooker?

A. For a stainless steel cavity use any oven cleaner suitable for stainless steel. If acrylic use a cream cleanser and nylon rough backed sponge pad.

2 *Q.* Should I remove the insulating mat when I am not using metal dishes?

A. Yes.

3 *Q.* Should I cook food directly on the insulating mat?

A. No. Use the trivet.

4 *Q.* Why is it that microwave cookery books give only approximate timings. Nothing seems explicit?

A. There are so many variables in all forms of microwave cookery: temperature of food; type and shape of dish; temperature of the oven cavity. Unfortunately there is still a considerable need for trial and error.

105 Q. Why do some foods of the same weight take
     longer to cook?

     A. If food is thick or chunky it will take longer
     than if in thinner, flatter portions, since
     microwaves have easier access to the food and n
     so much density to work through.

106 Q. If I find food is not cooked enough, can I p
     it back into the oven and give it more time?

     A. Yes. Better to undercook and test result whe
     first learning microwave cookery.

107 Q. Should I aim to undercook food just as I do
     when using an ordinary microwave oven?

     A. Yes, if using the microwave on full power or
     HIGH setting in conjunction with convected hot
     air.

108 Q. If I left food in the oven to cool after it had
     finished cooking, would it be overcooked?

     A. It depends upon the mode selected. On
     combination mode the heat from the cavity wou
     work on the food—so food could spoil. On
     Microwave mode the heat is generated inside the
     food and the oven cavity would not be hot so it
     would make no difference if food is left in the
     oven to cool.

109 Q. Is it necessary to cover food?

     A. Follow the manufacturers handbook. Auto-
     sensor food must be covered for the sensor to
     work and some standard microwave cooked food
     must also be covered.

110 Q. Can you smell the food being cooked?

     A. Yes. The oven baked food smells just the
     same but microwaved vegetables have less odour
     because of the reduction in cooking time and
     water used.

Q. Could I start-off food in the microwave oven, prior to barbecueing, to speed things up?

A. Yes, a good idea. Three-quarter cook everything! This will also prevent burning the outside of food on the barbecue, whilst still achieving the charcoal flavour.

2 *Q.* How can I stop milk boiling over?

A. Always use a jug or container of twice the capacity of the liquid measurement.

3 *Q.* Why is it necessary to have a cup of water in the microwave oven whilst drying herbs or melting plain chocolate?

A. Because there is insufficient moisture for the microwaves to be absorbed into, and this could result in damage to the microwave oven.

4 *Q.* Can I add salt to food as I usually do?

A. Yes, but never sprinkle salt directly onto food that is to be cooked on the microwave mode. It will attract the microwaves and overcook the food leaving unpleasant burn marks. Dissolve salt in liquid before adding to food.

5 *Q.* Can I use fat when roasting meat?

A. Yes. Use fat, lard or oil as a cooking medium; whichever is preferred.

6 *Q.* Can I warm plates in the microwave combination oven?

A. Yes. On convection setting.

7 *Q.* How is food kept hot whilst the next part of the meal is cooking?

A. It is unnecessary to keep food hot, as the microwave oven can be used as an instant warmer-upper prior to serving the completed dish.

118 Q. Should I leave the oven door open to allow
     to cool between dishes?

     A. A cooling fan is incorporated to assist the
     problem and is sufficient unless intending to c
     foods where correct temperature setting is criti
     Such foods should always be cooked first.

119 Q. As some foods, a stew for instance, take so
     long wouldn't it be quicker to use a pressure
     cooker.?

     A. A pressure cooker will cook stews quicker
     than the microwave; however, microwave cooki
     preserves nutrients and flavour, and at only a
     fraction of the cost of using a pressure cooker.

120 Q. How much food can be cooked at any one
     time?

     A. As much as the machine will hold but,
     remember, the larger the quantity the longer th
     cooking time.

121 Q. Can I stop the turntable to utilise the whole
     of the oven cavity?

     A. Check with the manufacturers handbook. T
     facility varies from one manufacturer to another

122 Q. Would it be possible to warm dishes ready
     serving?

     A. Yes. Using the convection mode.

123 Q. I am told that wine bottles may be sterilized
     in the microwave oven. How?

     A. Cleanse, rinse and dry bottles. Shake out an
     lay on their sides in the oven. Heat on HIGH
     setting until bottles are warm and dry—a few
     minutes only.

Q. Can I convert my own family conventional recipes?

A. The answer is yes you can, but there is no hard and fast rule. Each recipe has to be treated in a separate way. Eventually microwave cooking becomes instinctive.

Q. Where can I get help with cooking queries that are raised daily?

A. Microwave specialists throughout the country run cookery lessons, as do manufacturers. Some local radio stations have regular phone-in programmes.

Q. If I enrol in classes for microwave cooking, would the timings be correct for my oven?

A. Specific instructions for each class member's oven should be given.

Dishes

*The correct selection of dishes is essential
the performance of your oven and the
satisfactory results of the food. Suitability
dishes varies from machine to machine, so
check your manufacturers handbook for
further guidance.*

Q. Which dishes are most suitable for a combination oven?

A. Pyrex or earthenware as both can be used on any of the 3 modes.

8 Q. Is there a special microwave Pyrex?

A. Certain dishes have a microwave label on them but all Pyrex is suitable.

9 Q. What dishes can I use during the combination mode of convection and microwave?

A. Pyrex, pottery or earthenware are ideal for use with both and suitable for all combination ovens. Metal dishes can also be used if recommended by manufacturer.

30 Q. Since I can use metal dishes in my microwave convection oven, should I use foil to roast a chicken?

A. No. Open metal dishes can be used because there is still the top opening to allow microwave penetration in addition to hot air convection. If you wrapped a chicken in metal foil, the microwaves would not reach the food, and therefore food would be cooked only on convection as with a conventional cooker.

31 Q. What would happen if I did use metal dishes in microwave mode?

A. The microwaves would bounce off the dish so would be unable to cook food properly. It could also damage the machine.

32 Q. Can I use aluminium foil in the microwave oven?

A. Yes, but with caution, and in the opposite way to conventional cooking. Microwaves cannot penetrate metal so foil is used to prevent microwaves from cooking food, such as wing tips on a chicken, which may overcook if not protected. Never allow foil to touch any part of the microwave oven.

133   *Q.* Can I use plastic dishes on combination mode?

    A. Generally no but certain plastic microwave dishes available can safely be used in combinatic or convection modes to temperatures of 200°C (400°F).

134   *Q.* My instruction book suggests using dishes with a low thermal mass! What are such dishes?

    A. Clear or coloured oven-proof glassware and lightweight ceramics.

135   *Q.* Do the dishes get hot in a combination oven

    A. Yes. Direct heat is applied in the form of hot air distributed by a fan when using combination or convection modes.

136   *Q.* Why do I need a roasting rack?

    A. Microwaves work on moisture. If a joint of meat was cooked on a plate, part of the joint would be immersed in juices. The meat needs to be raised up to ensure even cooking.

137   *Q.* Can I use the metal rack from the combination cooker on the microwave mode also?

    A. Yes, but only if manufacturer recommends it

138   *Q.* Are there different types of roasting racks?

    A. Yes, but they all do the same job and only one is necessary.

139   *Q.* Should I use a rack for anything other than joints?

    A. Yes, for beefburgers, fish fingers, tomatoes, bacon.

40 Q. Can I use the roasting rack as a shelf when baking cakes?

A. Yes. It would assist even cooking.

41 Q. When I used my browning dish a dark stain appeared. Is it damaged?

A. No. It is not damaged but you have allowed the dish to become dirty by not cleaning properly after use every time.

42 Q. How do I clean a browning dish?

A. With cream cleanser and a nylon pot brush while the dish is still hot. Bicarbonate of Soda mixed to a paste with a little water also works well.

43 Q. When I used the browning dish exactly according to the manufacturer's instructions, the food didn't brown. Is the dish faulty?

A. Unlikely. Probably the instructions are. Add oil to the dish before heating. After preheat time the oil and dish are hot and crisp brown food should result.

44 Q. Is there danger if the browning dish is overheated?

A. Yes. Fat could ignite and the glass turntable could shatter.

45 Q. What is the advantage of using the lid on the browning dish?

A. It stops fat splashing and cooks food quicker, but will detract from the browning if used whilst frying foods.

46 Q. Should I use HIGH power whilst using the browning dish?

A. Heat the dish using HIGH power. Food can be cooked on MEDIUM/ROAST.

147 Q. Should I use a browning dish on combination setting?

A. No.

148 Q. Would I need a browning dish?

A. Not necessarily. Fat can be heated on a Pyrex tray on convection mode. However, a browning dish is the most successful method for frying eggs using the oven.

149 Q. Can I use a Pyrosil dish instead of a browning dish? It looks the same.

A No. The browning dish is a special type of dish with a metallic coated base-plate which reflects microwaves and heats up rapidly; unlike the Pyrosil dish which would remain cold.

150 Q. My family like fried foods. Which would be the best purchase, an electric frying-pan or a browning dish?

A. It depends entirely on your family needs. An electric frying pan could obviously be in use during the microwave cooking of other foods. Both give identical results.

151 Q. When I used my normal Pyrex dish and recipe for Yorkshire pudding, it overflowed. Why?

A. Food boils more rapidly in a microwave combination oven so it is necessary to use a deeper dish than in a conventional oven.

152 Q. When I used a roasting bag, it ballooned up. Would it alter the cooking time if I punctured it?

A. No. A small hole in the top is necessary.

153 Q. All the roasting bags that I have purchased have metal ties supplied. If I should not use them, what can I use?

A. Elastic bands or clear adhesive tape.

54 *Q.* When should I use roasting bags?

A. Roasting bags are most effective when roasting a joint of meat or poultry. The bag creates a self-basting effect, and aids browning.

55 *Q.* Are there special 'roasting' and 'boiling' bags especially for use in the microwave oven?

A. No. Use ordinary cooking bags.

56 *Q.* Can I use existing cake tins?

A. The specifications of combination ovens varies considerably. Some manufacturers provide suitable insulation in their ovens to enable metal dishes to be used during combination or convection modes.

57 *Q.* I have a collection of large paté dishes from the supermarket. Are such dishes suitable for use in the microwave oven?

A. Paté dishes are excellent.

58 *Q.* I bought special plastic microwave containers for cooking vegetables. There are no lids supplied and plastic wrap doesn't stick to them. What do I do?

A. Put a dinner plate on top when food needs to be covered during cooking.

59 *Q.* Can glass dishes be used for cooking?

A. Microwaves ignore every substance except metal and moisture, passing through every other material as light passes through a window. However, if water was poured into a glass then heated in the microwave to boiling point the glass would shatter due to the boiling water, not the microwaves. The temperature of the contents is the deciding factor.

160   *Q*. Is it all right to use bone china in a microwave oven?

     A. Yes, but not if it has gold or silver rimming or decoration. Remember that very hot food may crack delicate dishes.

161   *Q*. Is melamine a type of plastic, and should I use it?

     A. Melamine is a type of plastic, but no do not use in the microwave oven. It is porous and will become very hot during use and may distort.

162   *Q*. Is it suitable to use ironstone pottery?

     A. Yes. Ironstone is a name only given to style and does not contain metal.

163   *Q*. Which is the most useful dish to purchase?

     A. A three-piece dome-dish set complete with a rack and tray which, when turned upside down, provides a 2.3 litre (4pt) covered casserole dish. Check suitability for use in combination mode.

164   *Q*. Where can I buy microwave accessories?

     A. From department stores, microwave oven specialist and by mail order.

Defrosting

The combined use of a microwave oven and deep-freezer truly symbolizes the lifestyle of today. Never before has good food been so readily or quickly available!

165 *Q*. Do all microwave ovens defrost?

A. Yes. Some of the older machines do not have a DEFROST setting, but if the oven is switched on and off at 30 sec intervals, defrosting will be satisfactory.

166 *Q*. Can all foods be defrosted in the microwave oven?

A. Yes. Microwaves defrost quite naturally.

167 *Q*. What is the secret of successful defrosting?

A. Work by weight; at 650 watts allow 8 min per 450g (1lb.)

168 *Q*. Do all foods need to be completely defrosted prior to cooking, or can some foods be cooked from a frozen state?

A. All frozen vegetables may be cooked without prior defrosting, also beefburgers, small whole fish, fish fingers, fish cakes, fillets of fish, kippers.

169 *Q*. What would happen to the food if I defrosted on HIGH by mistake?

A. It would start to cook very unevenly around the outside, and food would be cooked at the edges but frozen solid in the centre.

170 *Q*. If I prepare a plated meal, can I freeze it?

A. Yes. To serve, reheat on HIGH setting without prior defrosting.

171 *Q*. Why does a square block of frozen food take so much longer to defrost than similar weight and type of food frozen in a larger flatter dish?

A. Microwaves have easier access to flatter dishes and do not have to work through food that is piled up or presented in a smaller deeper receptacle.

172   *Q*. Is it completely safe to defrost seafood using a microwave oven?

  A. Yes. Many restaurateurs deliberately use a microwave oven to ensure that food is sterilized.

173   *Q*. Is it necessary to defrost frozen vegetables before cooking?

  A. No. Follow microwave cooking instructions for fresh food, but allow half as much time additionally.

174   *Q*. The cookbook supplied with my machine suggests defrosting a chicken on a roasting rack placed on the turntable direct. Surely the water will overflow?

  A. No. Surprisingly enough there is very little water left after defrosting. Most of it evaporates during the process.

175   *Q*. Can I use the DEFROST setting to cook?

  A. Yes. It is useful for stews or slow cooking.

176   *Q*. How do I defrost frozen butter?

  A. Heat for 30 sec on DEFROST setting.

177   *Q*. Whenever I defrost a chicken in the microwave oven, the inside remains icy. If I persist and add more time, the outside starts to cook. How do I avoid this?

  A. Defrost according to the manual supplied with the machine. At the end of this time rinse the carcase with cold water and allow to stand on a rack for 8–10 min.

178   *Q*. Can I defrost fresh cream cakes?

  A. Yes, but exercise caution, using DEFROST setting for 30 sec–45 sec at a time.

179   *Q*. How should I defrost frozen pastry?

    A. With care! Use the DEFROST setting and check that pastry is not allowed to get even slightly warm.

180   *Q*. If I accidentally turned-on the cook button instead of DEFROST, and the chicken being defrosted started to cook, would it be safe to eat when cooked?

    A. Yes. Provided the poultry was completely cooked in the microwave oven. Food is sterilised during cooking.

Reheating

Traditionally, the thought of reheated food does not inspire the tastebuds. However, microwave reheated food is different because colour, texture and flavour all remain unaltered and the nutrients are retained.

181 *Q.* Should I use microwave or combination modes for reheating food?

A. Depending upon whether you want the food crispy. Sauces, vegetables, plate meals should be reheated on microwave. Large pies, pasties etc. on combination mode.

182 *Q.* How long will a plated meal take to reheat from the freezer?

A. Nothing varies so much as individual portions of family meals because like everything else connected with microwave cooking, weight is the important factor. Allow 5–9 min from frozen. Remember, better too hot than too cold. Food won't spoil if you add more time.

183 *Q.* What would happen to a plated meal if it were reheated more than once?

A. There would be little or no change and it would be edible. In practice this should not be necessary as a meal takes only a matter of minutes to heat precisely when required.

184 *Q.* When reheating a meal how would I get all the food in the oven in different shaped dishes?

A. You wouldn't. The easiest method would be to fill a large flattish dish then reheat all together, and serve from the dish. Alternatively, plate up individual meals and reheat.

185 *Q.* Should food be covered during reheating time?

A. This is unnecessary.

186 *Q.* When I reheated baked beans, they popped open and made a mess. Why?

A. Because you overheated them! The contents of a small tin takes only ½ min on HIGH setting.

187 Q. Can I put two plates of food in the oven at once to reheat?

A. Yes. There are purpose-made plastic ring-stackers available. Up to three meals may be heated at once.

188 Q. Can I reheat mince pies from the freezer?

A. Yes. Using HIGH setting, and allow 30–45 sec each from frozen. A plate of 6 pies will take 2½–3 min.

189 Q. When reheating soup I find it is always cold in the centre of the dish. Why?

A. The centre is always the last part to heat up. Stir once during cooking.

190 Q. Is it really quite safe to reheat pork in the microwave oven?

A. Everything that is cooked or reheated in the microwave is sterilised due to the intense heat that is generated inside the food.

191 Q. How long would it take to reheat a 2.3 litre (4pt) family-sized frozen casserole?

A. Allow 14–18 min on HIGH setting. Do not defrost first. Foods that have been cooked, then frozen, can quite safely be reheated on a HIGH setting. The DEFROST setting is important to use on frozen uncooked foods because of its pulsating action of switching on and off, thus ensuring that frozen foods do not start to cook on the outside whilst still frozen in the centre.

192 Q. Is it safe to reheat all leftovers?

A. Yes. Food is sterilized by the microwaves.

93 Q. Is it possible to reheat fish and chips, and should I remove the wrapper?

A. Fish and chips may be reheated in the paper.

194 *Q.* If I prepare a 'ready meal' and leave it in the fridge, the gravy soaks in. Should I reheat it separately?

A. Yes, for absolute perfection. I use ramekins for this purpose, and never waste any gravy at all. Gravy can be frozen and reheated.

195 *Q.* How long will it take to reheat a bought Christmas pudding?

A. Allow 3–4 min for a 450g (1lb) size, 5–6 min for a 900g (2lb) size.

196 *Q.* When I reheat ready cooked pastry it collapses and becomes soggy. Is there a remedy?

A. Pastry should be reheated for the absolute minimum of time. Always make a hole or two in the top of a pie to allow hot air to escape whilst heating. A knife blade does this effectively without spoiling the appearance. It will also assist if the pie is placed on an open roasting rack, allowing air to circulate underneath. For family-size pies use combination mode which would be uneconomical for small portions because of the pre-heat time needed.

197 *Q.* Could I leave a cooked English breakfast to reheat?

A. Yes, but fried egg should be left on a saucer separately. Heat breakfast for 1–2 min and egg for only 15–25 sec.

198 *Q.* Can I take the chill off my cat's food taken from the fridge?

A. Yes, 15 sec per portion maximum.

199 *Q.* How can I stop a skin forming on custard or sauce I wish to reheat later?

A. Place a circlet of dampened greaseproof paper on top of jug.

Meat and Poultry

Microwave cooked meat has been subjected to
considerable criticism in the past, generally
because of the pale unappetizing appearance.
Combination cooking presents succulent
crispy meat, with the added advantage of
very little loss through shrinkage.

200 *Q.* My microwave combination oven is supplied with a trivet that fits over the turntable. The instruction manual suggests utilizing the turntable to catch juices whilst roasting meats on the trivet. This works successfully, but means that the turntable needs emptying of juices and cleaning before I can reheat vegetables etc. by which time the meat has gone cold, how can I overcome this.

A. Use a large covered dish for roasting, such as the Corning chicken casserole. Place this on the turntable using the deepest dish as the base. Cook covered for half the required time. After the half way period, transfer meat to lid (upended), retaining the meat juices for gravy making. Cook the roast uncovered for the second period of time. This method also reduces cleaning to an absolute minimum.

201 *Q.* When roasting meats, which give the better result; combination or convection mode?

A. Both give identical results but combination is quicker.

202 *Q.* If microwaves cook from the inside out, how can I cook rare beef?

A. Microwaves do not cook from the inside out, but start at the outer edge of the food and work inwards. Food is cooked from within its own skin, which causes this confusion. Cooking rare beef is simple—just reduce the cooking time per 450g (1lb).

203 *Q.* Can I roast meat and potatoes together?

A. Yes. Calculate the time by total weight of food as shown in instruction manual.

204 *Q.* Is it possible to cook Yorkshire pudding in the microwave combination oven?

A. Yes. On combination mode. It is unnecessary to pre-heat fat; greasing the dish is all that is required.

205 *Q.* How would I cook a leg of lamb?

A. On the trivet or rack supplied. Obviously it would have to be halved if too large for the turntable to revolve.

206 *Q.* A recipe book suggests cooking a chicken inside a roasting bag, yet the manufacturer's instructions suggest using a rack. Which is best?

A. Both together! Place chicken in roasting bag; puncture holes in the bottom of the bag, stand bag on a roasting rack for cooking.

207 *Q.* Is it in order to put stuffing into poultry before roasting?

A. Yes. Calculate the cooking time per 450g (1lb) after stuffing the bird.

208 *Q.* Microwaved roasted meats do not shrink in size. Will this alter if using combination mode?

A. Yes. Unfortunately, the application of hot air to the food will certainly speed up the shrinkage as fat melts more rapidly.

209 *Q.* If I use stuffing in poultry, will it take longer to cook?

A. Yes. According to total weight.

210 *Q.* What is the spice that browns a chicken when using microwave-only mode?

A. Paprika is excellent, or there are purpose-made food colourings available.

211 *Q.* Is it possible to cook pheasant in the microwave oven?

A. Yes, unless there is a lot of buckshot visible there should be no problem. Cook as for chicken.

212 *Q.* When I cooked a turkey the meat around the leg was overcooked. How can this be avoided.?

A. The thinnest part gets the greatest concentration of microwaves. Covering wing tips and legs with aluminium foil. Do not allow foil to touch sides of oven.

213 *Q.* I have not yet seen a microwave browning oven large enough to take a Christmas turkey. How could I overcome the problem?

A. Most ovens take a 10lb turkey. Otherwise cook two turkeys or bone the turkey except for the legs. This makes a sensible proposition for a larger bird and is easier to carve.

214 *Q.* When I cooked liver it 'popped' and made a mess of the oven. Why?

A. Liver is covered with a membrane which, if not pierced before cooking, will expand and split. Simply prod liver with a fork prior to cooking.

215 *Q.* When making a steak and kidney pie, is it necessary to cook the meat first? If so, using which mode?

A. Yes. Use the microwave mode. Start on HIGH setting for 5 mins, then reduce setting to LOW/SIMMER, until meat is tender; approximately half conventional stewing time.

216 *Q.* Why does it take so long to cook steak and kidney?

A. Whilst meat takes a very short time to actually cook (until no juices show), cheaper cuts of meat require longer to tenderise, just as in conventional cooking.

17   *Q.* Why do some beefburgers cook quicker than others of the same weight, but of a different brand?

    A. Beefburgers and sausages contain cereals. Different brands have varying amounts of cereals and the higher the content of meat the longer the cooking time.

18   *Q.* When I cooked minced beef according to instructions supplied, it went into lumpy pieces. Is this normal?

    A. Yes, but can be overcome by breaking up with a fork during cooking.

19   *Q.* How should I cook sausages?

    A. Preheat oven on convection mode for 5 mins, place sausages on a greased pyrex pizza tray. Use combination mode with microwave set low and convection set high. Cook until sausages are brown and crisp. Use same method for simulating 'grilled' chops or steak.

20   *Q.* When I cooked rashers of bacon they were limp, pale and soggy, yet some I saw cooked at a demonstration were really brown and crispy. Why?

    A. Most probably the demonstration bacon was cooked on a rack. If rashers are cooked directly on a plate, fat cannot drain away from the bacon preventing it from becoming crisp.

21   *Q.* In the cookery book supplied with my machine it suggests cooking bacon on kitchen paper. I find it sticks.?

    A. Kitchen paper is fine to use provided the rashers are removed immediately the bell 'rings', otherwise time is spent trying to separate the bacon from paper. Try using a rack.

222   *Q*. How would you advise cooking savoury bacon rolls using a microwave oven?

A. Divide stuffing into 8 portions. Wrap each portion in a rasher, secure with a cocktail stick. Place savoury rolls on a roasting rack. Cook on HIGH setting for 8–10 min (makes 8).

223   *Q*. I am experiencing difficulty when cooking chops; they are always tough and dry?

A. Dryness means overcooking. Aim to cook until blood traces are almost gone. Remove from the microwave oven and, by the time you have served the remainder of the meal, the chops will have completed cooking from the heat within.

224   *Q*. Should I put oil in the browning dish before cooking chops?

A. Yes. Use 1–2×15ml tbsp (1–2 tbsp) and heat dish for 6–7 min.

225   *Q*. How would I thicken a stew?

A. Gravy granules are simple to use. Just sprinkle onto food and stir.

226   *Q*. Whenever I make gravy in the microwave, it forms lumps. Why?

A. The secret is in the mixing. Before adding the thickening agent to meat juices make sure that there are no particles of powder unmixed or, for an infallible result, use gravy granules.

Vegetables and Fruit

Fresh well-cooked vegetables are a fine source of vitamins and goodness, and excellent value for money. Microwave-cooked vegetables have superb flavour, are speedily cooked to retain even more nutrients, and cooking methods are very simple.

227 *Q.* Can I add salt to vegetables before cooking? My recipe book advises adding salt after cooking is completed?

A. Salt sprinkled directly onto vegetables would cause them to dehydrate and turn withered and brown. However, salt added to liquid and dissolved is a perfectly safe method.

228 *Q.* Are the nutrients still retained?

A. Yes. More so than with conventional cooking because of the speed of cooking and reduced amount of liquid used.

229 *Q.* Is it necessary to add water to frozen vegetables?

A. No. Unless large quantities are prepared together.

230 *Q.* Is it possible to blanch vegetables in the microwave combination oven?

A. Yes. Prepare vegetables; place in 1lb size boiling bags. Add 1 tablespoon of water to the bag; shake the water over the vegetables. Heat each bag for 2 mins using the microwave mode on HIGH setting. Cool the vegetables by plunging the bags up to the neck into iced water; seal and freeze in the usual way.

231 *Q.* My family like 'crunchy' vegetables, cooked in the French manner. Is the microwave oven capable of cooking such foods?

A. Yes. It is a simple matter of reducing the time per 450g (1lb) of food.

232 *Q.* Can I cook two vegetables together?

A. Yes, provided they are of the same type; eg parsnips and swede. Combined cooking of beans and carrots would not be possible. Generally there is no advantage in cooking vegetables together because microwaves take as long to cook together as if cooked separately.

233   *Q.* Then how do I keep the first hot?

     A. There is no need to. Food can be reheated as required without detriment to flavour or appearance.

234   *Q.* How long does it take to cook corn-on-the-cob using the microwave mode?

     A. It takes 3 min if fresh; 4 min if frozen. Brush the cobs with butter. There is no need to cover frozen cobs, but fresh ones will benefit from sealing inside plastic wrap.

235   *Q.* What is the best way to cook mushrooms?

     A. Prepare mushrooms and place in a dish with a knob of butter; seasoning and 1×15ml tbsp (1 tbsp) water. Cover and cook on HIGH for 3 min per 100g (¼ lb).

236   *Q.* What is the best way to cook cabbage?

     A. Shred cabbage and cook in a flattish container, covered, for 8–10 min per 450g (1lb). Halfway through cooking time, turn the bottom layers to the top of the dish.

37   *Q.* When I cooked minced beef with onions, the meat was completely cooked but the onions were crunchy? Did I do something wrong?

     A. No. Onions take quite a long time to soften when added to other foods. Start them off first for a couple of minutes.

38   *Q.* Carrots cooked in the microwave were unsatisfactory. The edges of the ones on top were rubbery, though the ones underneath were fine. Why?

     A. You should sprinkle water over the top of the vegetables prior to cooking.

239 *Q.* Whenever I cook cauliflower florets there are small black burn spots in places. Why is this and am I doing something wrong?

A. The small black burn spots appear on cauliflower when it is allowed to 'dry out'. This is easily rectified by sprinkling the water over the cauliflower prior to cooking. The moisture will protect the food from overheating in places.

240 *Q.* I boiled potatoes using the microwave oven, but it seemed to take longer than on the stove. Why?

A. You probably covered the potatoes with water, and this is unnecessary. 12–20mm (½–¾in) is all that is needed.

241 *Q.* I cannot master the art of cooking plain old-fashioned boiled potatoes; the result is always dried up edges and hard middles. How is it done?

A. Use a wide flattish dish so that the potatoes are spread over it instead of piled up. Cook to manufacturer's instructions, or on HIGH in 12–20mm (½–¾in) salted water. Before cooking commences, toss the water over the top of the potatoes making the tops wet. Always cover during cooking. If the dish has no lid a dinner plate will do.

242 *Q.* Can I cook new potatoes in skins the same way as boiled potatoes?

A. Yes. Cooking instructions are the same as for normal boiled potatoes.

243 *Q.* Can I cook oven chips in the combination oven?

A. Yes. Use the convection mode to heat up the oven for 5 mins. Spread chips across the tray or turntable. Use combination on 2–3 min bursts until chips are crisp.

244   *Q*. My family is very fond of potato croquettes, hash browns and all other potato-based convenience foods that I buy frozen. How would I cook such products in the microwave combination oven?

  A. Use combination mode. Place food on the rack supplied; brush with oil or other melted fat. Experiment with timing; sometimes browning is more satisfactory if oven is preheated by convection-only mode for 5 minutes prior to cooking.

245   *Q*. Can I dry herbs?

  A. Yes. Put herbs between two sheets of kitchen paper. Always put an eggcupful of water in the machine whilst drying herbs.

246   *Q*. Is it simple to make apple sauce using the microwave oven?

  A. Yes. Core and score around middle of a large cooking apple. Cook in a deep cereal bowl for 3–4 min on HIGH. When cooked, scoop out centre, sweeten and serve. For larger quantities peel and slice as usual.

247   *Q*. How would I bake an apple in the microwave oven?

  A. Core and score skin around middle. Fill centre with granulated sugar and cook for 3–4 min on HIGH.

248   *Q*. What would happen if I didn't score an apple around middle before baking?

  A. Heat would build up from inside and the skin would burst making a mess in the oven.

49   *Q*. Could I fill an apple with sweet mincemeat before cooking?

  A. Yes. Alternatively, use chopped dates and walnuts, blackberries and other soft fruit in season.

250 *Q.* A 'quick tip' in my microwave cookbook suggests warming a lemon to make it more juicy. For how long?

A. For 30–45 sec on HIGH; or until warm.

251 *Q.* Can I cook chestnuts in the microwave oven?

A. Yes. Score through skin around middle of each chestnut. Place on a plate or directly on turntable and cook for 6–7 min per 450g (1lb.)

252 *Q.* Can I brown almonds in the microwave oven?

A. Yes. Place on a rack between two sheets of kitchen paper. Put an eggcupful of water in the centre of the rack. Microwave on HIGH until almonds turn brown.

253 *Q.* I make jam and marmalade in my microwave oven. Will I still be able to do so in a microwave combination oven?

A. Yes, using the microwave-only mode.

Baking and Puddings

Making cakes and puddings is a simple process in the microwave oven. But be warned; there is no legitimate excuse for ever buying cakes and puddings again! This section is ideal for introducing the family to microwave cooking.

254 *Q*. Why should I use the convection mode for baking small cakes?

A. Because if the combination setting was used, the microwaves would cook the cakes in 10–20 sec each, not allowing the convected hot air time to brown them.

255 *Q*. When I use a muffin pan lined with paper cases for small cakes, the base gets wet and the cake becomes soggy. What can I do about it?

A. Use two paper cases rather than one, and turn cakes out immediately.

256 *Q*. If I leave my cake to stand, in accordance with the recipe instructions, there is a white gluey-looking film around the base when I turn it out of the container. Why?

A. The film you mention is usually in evidence when using a plastic container. To rectify, leave to stand for 2–3 min only.

257 *Q*. Should I turn cakes out immediately or leave them to stand in the dish?

A. Cakes should be left in the dish for a few minutes before turning out.

258 *Q*. If I open the microwave oven door during the cooking of a cake, will it shrink?

A. No. There is sufficient heat within the cake to hold its shape for several seconds.

259 *Q*. When making cakes is it necessary to grease and flour dishes?

A. Grease only.

260 *Q*. Will a sponge cake brown?

A. Yes. Combination or convection mode both give good results.

1   *Q.* Should I bake a Victorian Sponge on combination or convection mode?

    A. Combination is quicker. Microwave should be set LOW.

2   *Q.* Can I cook the two halves of a Victoria sponge together; with one half on the rack and the other on the turntable?

    A. Yes.

3   *Q.* Can I heat jam for spreading, using the microwave oven?

    A. Yes. In the jar with lid removed. Heat for 30 sec intervals on HIGH.

4   *Q.* Can I melt chocolate in the microwave oven?

    A. Break a 225 (8oz) bar of milk chocolate into small pieces into a dish and add approximately 1×15ml tbsp (1tbsp) milk. Heat on HIGH setting for approximately 1 min. Stir thoroughly. If plain chocolate—melt alone—but stand 1 eggcupful of water on the turntable.

5   *Q.* My microwave browning cooker has a minimum convection setting of 160°. How can I make meringues?

    A. By using the microwave mode.

6   *Q.* Some books say that pancakes can be made in the microwave oven; others say they can't. Which is true?

    A. Pancakes can be cooked in the microwave oven, but a browning dish is necessary.

7   *Q.* How can I cook dumplings?

    A. Mix your favourite recipe and add to hot cooked stews and casseroles. Cook for 5 min on HIGH.

268 *Q.* Can I cook a pizza?

A. Yes. Use combination mode.

269 *Q.* Is it possible to cook pastry in a microwave combination oven?

A. All pastries are very successful using combination or convection mode.

270 *Q.* Is it necessary to bake pastry first for a quiche?

A. No. The pastry cooks and seals very quickly so it is not necessary.

271 *Q.* Is it possible to 'prove' bread?

A. Yes. In 30 sec bursts on HIGH until dough doubles in size.

272 *Q.* Is it possible to bake bread using the microwave combination oven?

A. Yes. Microwave baked bread is quite successful.

273 *Q.* Can I warm bread rolls prior to serving?

A. Yes. For 30 sec on HIGH. Serve immediately.

274 *Q.* I have heard that steamed sponge puddings are absolutely superb when cooked in a microwave oven. Do I cover the top and stand the dish in water?

A. No. On both counts. Mix the pudding in a basin; stand it on the turntable. Cook on HIGH for 5 min uncovered.

275 *Q.* Do I ever have to cover the top of the basin when cooking steamed puddings?

A. Yes. If you were making a suet pudding the top would require covering and the whole basin sealed into plastic wrap with a slit made in the top.

6 *Q.* Why, when I cooked a sponge pudding did it overflow although I used the recommended size of dish?

A. Microwaves have the ability to make puddings and cakes rise very high. Often larger dishes are necessary. In the case of a pudding bowl, I use a 1.1 litre (2pt) rather than a 1kg (2lb). It makes all the difference.

7 *Q.* Why does rice pudding rise up and down during cooking?

A. Because it is cooked using a LOW setting. To simulate a thermostat the machine switches on and off for preset times. eg. SIMMER microwave is on for 20 sec and off for 40 sec in every minute. The rice pudding rises when the machine is on for 20 sec, drops again when the machine 'rests' for 40 sec.

8 *Q.* I saw a demonstrator make a Saucy Sponge from a packet. How long does it take to bake?

A. Approximately 5–6 min on HIGH. Mix exactly as packet instructions. Use only one dish.

9 *Q.* Which is the correct mode for cooking a roly-poly?

A. Microwave.

30 *Q.* Is it necessary to cover suet roly-poly?

A. Yes. Loosely wrap roly-poly in greaseproof paper; then wrap in plastic wrap leaving room for mixture to rise.

31 *Q.* Whenever I make custard it boils over. Why?

A. It will unless a large jug is used. All milk-based foods boil rapidly in the microwave oven and it is better to use a 1.1 litre (2pt) jug for 550ml (1pt) of custard.

282 *Q.* Is it possible to make smooth non-lumpy custard in the microwave?

A. Yes. The secret is in the mixing stage. Mix custard powder, sugar and top of milk extra thoroughly, before adding remaining milk. A 550ml (1pt) mixture takes approximately 5–6 m on HIGH setting.

283 *Q.* Could I make Baked Alaska using the microwave combination oven?

A. Yes. On convection mode.

284 *Q.* Can I use my Christmas Pudding recipe in the microwave oven?

A. Yes. Cook on HIGH for 5–6 min for 450g (1l size; 8–9 min for 900g (2lb) size.

Fish

*There is simply no better way of cooking fish
than in a microwave oven. Goodness, texture
and flavour are all retained, and the cooking
odours are contained in the oven.*

285   *Q.* I have tried to microwave fish but it does not cook in the centre. Why?

     A. Covering the dish will ensure even cooking.

286   *Q.* My microwave oven cooks fish superbly. My only complaint is the smell left inside the oven after cooking. How can I freshen-up the machine?

     A. Cut a juicy lemon in half. Using both halves, rub round the oven cavity. Leave for a few seconds before drying thoroughly with a paper towel. If smell persists, repeat the process.

287   *Q.* How would I cook a large whole fish? It would fit on the turntable but not turn around?

     A. You could cook the fish using microwave-only mode. If your machine has a stirrer fan, the turntable plate can be removed, upturned or stopped (depending on the machine). Cook the fish as recipe states, turning manually twice. If your machine does not have an oven-sited fan, the fish would have to be filleted.

288   *Q.* How can I cook a frozen trout?

     A. Cooked from raw or frozen on HIGH setting, a 225g (8oz) trout will take 4 min. If preferred cook on HIGH for 1 min to start defrosting, then stuff the trout or add garnish. Continue cooking for 3 min or until cooked through.

289   *Q.* Is it possible to cook whitebait in the microwave oven?

     A. Yes, by using a browning dish. Heat dish with 1×15ml tbsp (1tbsp) oil on HIGH for 5–6 min; add prepared fish and cook for 5–6 min per 450g (1lb), turning once. Alternatively by heating fat or oil on convection, then cooking on combination setting until fish is crisp.

290 *Q.* Can I pot shrimps using the microwave oven?

A. Butter a ramekin; add prepared shrimps and season to taste. Put a knob of butter on top. Heat on HIGH for 30 sec or until butter melts. Leave to set. Garnish with parsley before serving.

291 *Q.* How would I cook fish fingers?

A. Place between two plates; one acting as a lid. Cook for 30 sec each if defrosted; 45 sec each if frozen, on HIGH setting. Several may be cooked at once. Alternatively cook as for whitebait (see question 289).

292 *Q.* Can I cook breaded fish using the microwave oven?

A. Yes. Brush the portions with oil or melted fat and cook on combination mode.

293 *Q.* When using bought frozen cod steaks in a sauce, is it necessary to remove the plastic wrapping bags before cooking?

A. No. Slit the corner of the plastic packaging and cook the whole packet on a plate with a raised edge.

294 *Q.* Is it possible to cook kippers in a microwave oven?

A. Yes, and very successfully. Place kippers in a dish; dot each kipper with margarine or butter; cover and cook on HIGH setting for 4–5 min per 450g (1lb).

295 *Q.* Do you recommend cooking scampi in a microwave oven, or should I cook it conventionally?

A. Small amounts of scampi can be cooked in the same manner as breaded fish. (See question 292) Large family-sized quantities should be cooked conventionally in deep fat.

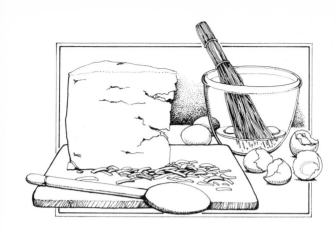

Eggs and Cheese

Eggs and cheese form the basis of many recipes, and are valuable for nutrients as well as distinctive flavour. Use in recipes as you would conventionally.

296 *Q.* How do eggs become 'scrambled' when cooked in a microwave oven?

A. Using HIGH setting first melt butter, before adding beaten eggs and milk. Stir once only during cooking, and the eggs magically scramble themselves when finally stirred after cooking is complete. Two eggs take approximately $1\frac{1}{2}$ min.

297 *Q.* Can I add salt to scrambled eggs before cooking?

A. Yes.

298 *Q.* Why do cookbooks suggest using a Pyrex jug for scrambled eggs?

A. Because its handle helps when stirring during cooking, and because Pyrex is clear, enabling the egg mixture to be watched since it is important not to overcook.

299 *Q.* Would scrambled eggs cook successfully in the microwave oven if I added 50g (2oz) cheese?

A. Perfectly. Alternatively try also adding crumbled cooked streaky bacon.

300 *Q.* Is it possible to fry an egg in a microwave browning oven?

A. Yes. Using a browning dish. Heat 1×15ml tbsp (1tbsp) oil on HIGH for $3-3\frac{1}{2}$ min. Break egg into hot fat. Cook for 15-20 sec on HIGH setting.

301 *Q.* Most cookbooks warn against boiling eggs in a microwave oven but is it *possible*?

A. Yes, but rather impractical. Wrap the egg in aluminium foil and immerse in a small basin of water. Heat water for approx $3\frac{1}{2}$ min on HIGH setting.

302   *Q.* Why do poached eggs explode?

A. Any food that has a skin will explode if heated too much. Though some books recommend it, I never 'pierce' eggs. Try using 1×15ml tbsp (1tbsp) water and a few drops of vinegar or ½×5ml tsp(½tsp) margarine or butter. Heat on HIGH for 30 sec; add egg, then microwave on HIGH for 30 sec.

303   *Q.* Could I bake an egg custard?

A. Yes. Using a bain marie or improvise with two different sized pyrex dishes.

304   *Q.* Can I melt cheese for topping toast using a microwave oven?

A. Yes. Slice amount of cheese required onto a plate. Microwave on HIGH setting until it melts.

305   *Q.* Is it possible to make French-loaf pizzas, topped with cheese, using the microwave oven for the whole process?

A. Yes. Prepare bread with cheese on top use combination setting. (Convection HIGH microwave LOW) for approx 4 min each pizza.

Pasta, Rice and Cereal

Whilst there is minimal time-saving in certain areas of cooking the above foods, results are superb and the methods clean and convenient–not to mention the lack of washing up after! Boiling water in a kettle first will speed the cooking process considerably.

306   *Q.* I cooked long-grained rice and it boiled over leaving a sticky mess. Where did I go wrong?

       A. Use a 2.3 litre (4pt) container to allow for bubbling up. If you have variable power, reduce to MEDIUM setting after water boils.

307   *Q.* I find that it takes too long to cook rice in the microwave oven. Are there any short cuts?

       A. Boil water first in an electric kettle.

308   *Q.* How should I cook egg noodles?

       A. For 225g (8oz) of noodles you will need a 4pt covered dish and 556ml (1pt) boiling salted water. Cook on HIGH setting for 5 min.

309   *Q.* Can I make porridge in a cereal bowl in the microwave oven?

       A. Yes, but make sure that the dish is deep enough as milk-based foods boil rapidly.

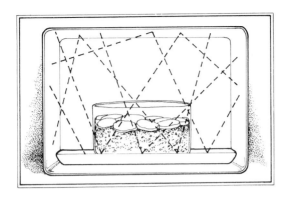

For the Technically Minded

Everyone, likes to know a little about 'How it Works'. Here then is a section to satisfy the most enquiring mind.

310 *Q.* Where does the heat come from?

A. From two sources. Hot air is circulated by a fan around the oven interior from the convection element. Microwaves agitate the molecules of moisture from within food which causes heat. A microwave combination oven can be programmed to use either source or in combination—hence the name.

311 *Q.* There is a protrusion at the base of my oven that almost touches the work surface. What is it?

A. It is an air-intake point for circulation.

312 *Q.* Why does the fan still continue to work after the machine has stopped cooking?

A. To assist the oven to cool down prior to cooking the next dish, thus allowing foods of different temperatures to be cooked in any order.

313 *Q.* Are touchmatic controls more accurate than manual?

A. Yes, but only because of human error using manual machines. Electronic controls eliminate this problem.

314 *Q.* When I used the metal rack supplied with my oven, it sparked inside the cavity so I have not used it since. The instructions state quite clearly that it is suitable for use on all modes. Why did it happen?

A. Only a microwave engineer will be able to answer. A possibility is that one of the ceramic insulating 'feet' is damaged. Do not use the rack until it has been checked.

315 *Q.* Can the turntable be stopped at all?

A. On certain machines, but only on certain modes, check instruction book or ask retailer prior to purchase.

316 Q. If microwaves pass through lids of dishes, why is it necessary to cover food?

A. Heat builds up inside the covered dish and food cooks quicker and retains moisture. Also, the oven stays clean.

317 Q. I leave a cup of water in my standard microwave oven at all times. Would I need to do this in the microwave combination oven?

A. Yes. In case the microwave browning oven was inadvertently switched on using the microwave mode. This is a safeguard to protect the machine from being used when empty which could damage the magnetron.

318 Q. If I cook food in a pudding basin, will it take longer than in a casserole dish?

A. Yes, as there is no lid to a pudding basin, and also because its greater depth to area causes food to be piled up. Microwaves will take longer to penetrate.

319 Q. When I cook a casserole the dish becomes very hot; yet if I use the same dish for warming up cooked food, it remains cool. Why?

A. Dishes are heated by food, not by microwaves; therefore if food is intensely hot over a relatively long period, dishes will become hot too.

320 Q. What is the seal?

A. It is the rectangular metal framing the glass in the door. Metal is the only substance that microwaves cannot penetrate.

321 Q. Is it possible for microwaves to leak out from around the door after lots of use?

A. Unlikely. The experts rate the chances of radiation harm from a microwave oven as the same as getting a suntan from the moon.

322   *Q*. What would happen if overspills got into the turntable mechanism?

    A. This is very unlikely as the glass tray holds 550ml (¾pt) of liquid.

323   *Q*. Is it normal for steam to be seen escaping from the door edge during the microwave cook-cycle?

    A. Yes, and it is perfectly safe and acceptable for this to happen. Microwaves cannot escape with the steam as they only travel in straight lines.

324   *Q*. I note from the specification of my appliance that the machine is 650 watts microwave part; 1.3kw convection. What fuse should I use?

    A. Whilst the output of your oven is only 650 watts the input could be as much as 1.4kw, therefore it is essential that you use a 13amp fuse.

325   *Q*. I can see the interior light through the sides of the door. Is the microwave safe?

    A. Yes. Microwaves cannot pass from the oven through a space in the door that small.

326   *Q*. If I break the glass turntable can it be replaced?

    A. The plate is easily obtained from microwave stockists.

327   *Q*. Can I replace the insulating mat?

    A. Yes. From microwave stockists or the manufacturer.

328   *Q*. If I set the timer for 10 min then open the door after 5 min, will I need to reset the timer?

    A. No. The timer is arrested and will not start again until the 'start' operation is touched.

29 *Q.* My microwave oven is a manual type machine. Using a time switch, could I programme it for the machine to switch on in my absence?

A. Yes. Set the machine up and press the starter. At pre-set time the microwave will start to cook, then switch itself off after cooking.

330 *Q.* My microwave oven has a clock. Does it matter if the machine is unplugged when not in use, and the clock is not set to proper time at each use?

A. No, since timing will still register the minutes selected regardless of the time of day.

331 *Q.* My cookbook mentions molecular activity. What is it?

A. It simply means the microwaves' movement through food.

332 *Q.* Is it possible to use the microwave oven without the turntable?

A. Yes, but only if the machine has a stirrer fan in the roof to turn the microwaves in the absence of the turntable. Otherwise it would be necessary to turn the dish manually during cooking.

333 *Q.* Why is the inside of the microwave oven made of metal if I may not use metal dishes?

A. Microwaves bounce off metal, therefore it reflects the waves into the food to be cooked.

334 *Q.* Why do some microwave ovens have a metal turntable?

A. Generally speaking, a metal turntable is supplied with convection ovens where glass or ceramic would break under extreme heat.

335   *Q.* What happens when the lightbulb burns out? Does the machine still work? Who replaces it and how?

     A. The lightbulb's function is purely to illuminate the cavity during cooking and does not affect the efficiency of the oven. It is advisable to have an experienced microwave engineer fit the replacement bulb. Check with your warranty, because the turntable plate and bulb are rarely covered. Some additional warranty premiums cover everything, and these are generally available from microwave specialists rather than from department stores.

336   *Q.* My microwave browning oven is noisy when the door is open, but my friend's is not. What is the difference?

     A. Some machines have a fan that works as soon as the door opens. Others only operate when the start button is touched.

337   *Q.* How far into the food do microwaves penetrate?

     A. About 15 to 20mm ($\frac{1}{2}$–$\frac{3}{4}$in) only.

338   *Q.* What does the magnetron do?

     A. It is one of the major components in any microwave oven. Its function is to pass microwaves into the metal cavity.

339   *Q.* What are cold spots?

     A. Parts of the microwave oven which do not get as much concentration of microwaves as others.

340   *Q.* Do all ovens have cold spots?

     A. Not any more. The efficiency of the stirrer fan and turntable combined has largely eliminated them.

41 *Q.* If I really overcooked food and dried it up completely, would it damage the oven?

A. In an extreme case, but only if food is totally dehydrated.

42 *Q.* Where does the microwave heat come from?

A. Microwaves, when passed through food, cause activity in the moisture molecules of the food. The intense activity creates friction—friction creates heat which cooks the food.

43 *Q.* When I need to use the timer on my manually operated microwave oven, the timer doesn't work on 30 sec. Why?

A. On manual timers it is necessary to turn the timer past 3 min then back to 30 sec.

44 *Q.* In the instruction manual supplied with my combination oven it clearly states not to use metal during the 'microwave' mode. Yet supplied with the machine is a metal rack for cooking meat that the manufacturers state is suitable. Why?

A. The rack you mention has ceramic insulators attached to the base, making it suitable for use.

45 *Q.* I have an old microwave cookbook which mentions equalizing time. What is it?

A. Standing time.

46 *Q.* What is standing time?

A. The heat generated inside the food is so intense that even after the machine is switched off, food still cooks from within. Experience soon tells when standing is beneficial.

Also Available

BEGINNING MICROWAVE COOKERY

Margaret Weale

Microwave cookery is different. Understanding an accepting this simple statement will prevent tears of frustration for the new microwave cook. Though most buyer of microwave ovens are experienced cooks who want learn the new techniques quickly and without failure many of the cookbooks available make easy learning difficult by having long and complicated explanations of the theory of microwave energy. Few read them properly an anyway soon forget. The recipes assume this knowledge and important steps for the inexperienced are left out with disappointing results.

This book is different. Margaret Weale has many year of experience of microwave cooking as a wife and moth and also as a home economist with a leading oven manufacturer. She has recognised the needs of the new microwave oven owner and arranged the chapters so that simp beginnings ensure successful result from the outset. Eac recipe is complete and reminds the cook of the essenti do's and don'ts. The step-by-step instructions leav nothing to chance and the charts on Defrosting, Reheatir and Freezer to Table are invaluable.

The author has test-cooked every recipe and supervise the colour photographs taken by her husband Stan.

Colour photographs throughout

£3.95 net

ISBN 0 948432 05 5

ANGELL EDITIONS
Newton Abbot, Devon